Night's Enigmatic Journey

In shadows deep, the silence sings,
A tapestry of hidden things.
Stars twinkle with a mystic flare,
Guiding dreams through midnight air.

Whispers ride on cool night's breeze,
Secrets shared among the trees.
Moonlight dances on the ground,
Casting spells without a sound.

The world transforms in twilight's grasp,
Mysterious hands in darkness clasp.
Footsteps echo through the glow,
Where time stands still, and wonders flow.

Each heartbeat thrums beneath the skies,
As the night unveils its guise.
Journey forth, let spirits play,
In night's embrace, we lose our way.

The Symphony of Midnight's Breath

In the hush of night, stars align,
Whispers of dusk, a soothing sign.
Moonlight dances on silken streams,
As shadows awaken, weaving dreams.

Gentle notes of the night sky play,
A melody soft, guiding the stray.
Each heartbeat echoes in the dark,
While silence cradles every spark.

Starlit Journeys Within

Beneath the cloak of heaven's glow,
The soul embarks on paths to sow.
Winds of wonder whisper and swirl,
As stardust paints the mind's bright world.

Each journey forged by moonlit dreams,
A tapestry sewn with silver beams.
Through galaxies where hopes entwine,
A voyage deep, where hearts align.

Chasing Dreams in the Void

In the vastness where shadows loom,
Dreams ignite, dispelling gloom.
Through cosmic realms, we take our flight,
Chasing visions in the night.

With every star, a wish set free,
In the silence, we find the key.
Boundless echoes, a hopeful song,
In the void, where we belong.

Hushed Tales of the Darkened Realm

In twilight's grasp, secrets reside,
Hushed whispers of time, a timeless tide.
Spirits dance in the silent air,
Through shadows deep, they wander and share.

With every flicker of candlelight,
Stories emerge from the heart of night.
Ancient echoes softly call,
In the darkened realm, we hear them all.

Threads of Cosmic Fantasy

In the silence of night's embrace,
Stars shimmer bright in infinite space.
Galaxies spin, weaving tales untold,
In the depths of the universe, dreams unfold.

From a whisper of stardust, stories spring,
Every twinkle a song, a celestial ring.
Across the dark canvas, colors ignite,
A tapestry of wonder, the cosmos in flight.

Serenity in the Depths of Dusk

Under the twilight, day softly fades,
Shadows grow long, where silence pervades.
Gentle whispers in the cool evening air,
Nature's calm heartbeat, a moment to share.

As stars awaken, they twinkle with grace,
The moon casts a glow, illuminating space.
In this tranquil hour, worries release,
Finding solace in dusk, a moment of peace.

Constellations of Hidden Dreams

In the quiet of night, wishes take flight,
Mapping the cosmos, dreams shine so bright.
Each star a beacon, hope in the dark,
Guiding lost souls to where dreams leave a mark.

Through the veil of clouds, visions appear,
Whispers of starlight, soft messages clear.
With every heartbeat, the universe beams,
Connecting the dots of our hidden dreams.

The Embrace of Mysterious Shadows

In the dance of twilight, shadows collide,
As night wraps the earth, like a blanket of pride.
Secrets are whispered in the cool evening light,
Mysterious shadows take wing in the night.

Through the thicket and trees, they silently roam,
Guardians of dreams, far away from home.
Embracing the unknown, they shadow our fears,
In the spectral ballet, the night gently clears.

Celestial Secrets of the Night

In shadows deep, the stars appear,
Whispering tales for those who hear.
The moonlight dances, soft and bright,
Unveiling secrets of the night.

Constellations weave their lore,
Guiding wanderers to distant shores.
With every twinkle, stories unfold,
Of ancient wonders, brave and bold.

A breeze that sings of distant dreams,
In night's embrace, nothing's as it seems.
The heavens watch with curious eyes,
As souls embark to touch the skies.

So linger here, where magic blends,
The night is young, and story never ends.

Reveries on the Edge of Dreams

Upon the cusp where visions lie,
Reality shifts, and shadows sigh.
In twilight's glow, our spirits weave,
A tapestry of hope to believe.

Illusions bloom like evening blooms,
Filling our hearts with whispered tunes.
Each thought takes flight on gossamer wings,
In the realm where fantasy sings.

Here in the hush, we drift and soar,
Beyond the world, to the evermore.
With every heartbeat, possibilities gleam,
In reveries that spark the dream.

Let go the day, embrace the night,
In silent realms, we find our light.

Nighttime Tales from the Other Side

Stories linger in the dark,
Echoes whisper, leaving a mark.
Phantom figures dance and glide,
Tales of wonder from the other side.

With every rustle and every sound,
The mysteries of dusk abound.
From hidden realms, the shadows speak,
Of love and loss, of strong and weak.

A lantern flickers, guiding the way,
Into the night, where spirits play.
With open hearts, we dare to roam,
In nighttime tales, we find our home.

So sit awhile, and hear them call,
For every story unfolds for all.

The Allure of Dusk's Embrace

When day departs, and colors fade,
Dusk reveals a serenade.
Soft hues blend in twilight's grace,
A gentle kiss, the world's embrace.

The sky ignites with shades of fire,
In soft selection, hearts aspire.
With each breath, the night draws near,
An invitation for dreams to steer.

Cascading stars like whispers fall,
Dusk's allure enchants us all.
In every sigh, a promise waits,
To unveil the wonders our heart creates.

Embrace the night, let worries cease,
In dusk's soft glow, we find our peace.

Dreams Adrift on a Midnight Sea

Whispers ride on waves so deep,
Drifting visions, secrets keep.
Stars above, they softly gleam,
Guiding souls through night's sweet dream.

Echoes of the tides resound,
In this realm, peace is found.
Moonlit paths where shadows play,
Awake the slumbering bay.

Each tear and laugh, a story spun,
Underneath the watchful sun.
Drifting souls in silver light,
Live the magic of the night.

The Lure of Twilight's Enigma

Colors blend as day departs,
Mysterious dance of hearts.
In the dusk, secrets reside,
Where the shadows briefly hide.

Endless dreams begin to bloom,
In the twilight's velvet gloom.
Fading echoes, soft and low,
Guide the weary hearts to flow.

In this haze, a promise sings,
Hope suspended on silent wings.
As twilight whispers, time stands still,
Cradling each unspoken thrill.

Chronicles of the Night's Serenity

Softly speaks the night divine,
In its depths, our dreams align.
With each breath, the stillness grows,
Nurtured by the moonlit prose.

Stars unfold their tales so bright,
As we wander through the night.
Holding time, so sweetly rare,
In this realm, we shed our care.

Gentle sighs of evening's song,
Where the restless hearts belong.
In the silence, wisdom gleams,
Weaving softly through our dreams.

The Secret Language of Stars

Among the stars, a language flows,
A truth that only night bestows.
Whispers crafted in cosmic light,
Sharing stories, dark and bright.

Galaxies spin their tales of old,
In silver streams, their secrets told.
Each twinkle, a note in the vast score,
A reminder of so much more.

Wishes made on falling stars,
Carried softly from afar.
In this language, hearts confide,
As we sail the night, side by side.

Dreams Woven in Midnight Hues

In the depths where shadows play,
Whispers dance, then fade away.
Stars unfold their silver threads,
Weaving stories in our heads.

Softly glows the moonlit stream,
Carrying every lost dream.
In twilight's arms, we softly sigh,
As hopes take flight and gently fly.

Each secret held within the night,
Lurks in corners out of sight.
Colors blend as hearts ignite,
Woven deep in dreams' delight.

Embrace the magic, let it flow,
Underneath the starlit glow.
In these hours, the soul takes flight,
Chasing dreams till morning light.

The Quietude of Nightfall

Night drapes silence, soft and deep,
As the world begins to sleep.
Crickets sing their lullabies,
As shadows stretch beneath the skies.

The breeze whispers through the trees,
Carrying scents of distant seas.
Moonbeams cast a peaceful glow,
Guiding thoughts to places low.

Clouds drift by, a gentle sight,
Embraced within the cloak of night.
Time slows down, we find our peace,
In night's embrace, our worries cease.

Stars awaken, twinkling bright,
Filling the dark with pure delight.
In quietude, our hearts find rest,
In the stillness, we are blessed.

Nighttime's Enchanted Murmurs

Beneath the stars, a story breathes,
In each rustle of the leaves.
Murmurs weave through cool night air,
Secrets shared without a care.

Flickering light, the fireflies play,
Guiding dreams that drift away.
Soft echoes of the night unfold,
Whispers of love yet to be told.

In the dark, the world feels new,
Every heartbeat, every view.
Surrounded by this midnight grace,
We disappear to find our place.

Through enchanted woods, we roam,
Finding in shadows, a whispered home.
In each murmur, life's refrain,
We dance in night, free of pain.

Silhouettes in the Twilight Mist

Mist wraps the world in a gentle guise,
As day fades softly, the dusk complies.
Silhouettes dance on the fading light,
In the arms of twilight, we feel the night.

Branches sway with a silent hum,
While fading colors softly succumb.
Echoes of laughter, tales of yore,
Fill the air as we yearn for more.

The horizon blurs in soft decay,
As shadows gather, holding sway.
Time drifts slowly, moments blend,
In twilight's mist, where dreams extend.

Hearts entwined in soft embrace,
With every heartbeat, we find our place.
Silhouettes linger in memory's kiss,
In twilight's fold, we find our bliss.

Tales from the Silver Hour

In twilight's glow, shadows play,
Whispers of stories, fading away.
Lost in the dance of the silver light,
Time weaves tales of day and night.

Stars awaken, secrets unfold,
Ancient legends, softly told.
Each flicker a moment, pure and rare,
In this hour, dreams fill the air.

Echoes of laughter, echoes of tears,
Visions of hopes across the years.
The silver hour, a canvas bright,
Painting the past in soft moonlight.

Chords of the Quiet Universe

Beneath the hush of a starlit sky,
Silent melodies begin to sigh.
Strings of the cosmos softly hum,
In this stillness, the heartbeats drum.

Galaxies spin in harmonious flight,
Chords of the quiet, pure delight.
Each twinkle a note in the grand design,
Binding the universe, yours and mine.

Whispers of comets, the breeze of a star,
Unseen connections, stretching afar.
In the vastness, we find our place,
Chords of love in this endless space.

Night's Gentle Embrace

The moon spills silver on sleeping streets,
Where shadows and silence softly meet.
Night's gentle arms wrap the world tight,
Cradling wishes in the soft twilight.

Stars blink lazily, secrets to share,
Guardians of dreams in the cool night air.
A hush unfolds, the wild winds cease,
In night's gentle embrace, we find peace.

Resting beneath the celestial dome,
In darkness, we wander, we feel at home.
Each glittering star, a fleeting grace,
In night's gentle embrace, we find space.

The Horizon Between Dream and Reality

Where dreams take flight and reality bends,
A horizon glimmers, where each journey begins.
The sun and moon in a tender chase,
Bridging the realms of time and space.

Wishes are woven in the twilight glow,
Breath of the universe, soft winds flow.
Each moment a thread in the tapestry fine,
We dance on the edge, where stars align.

Between the shadows, the whispers reside,
Secrets of life where doubts slide.
In the twilight's glow, we find our way,
At the horizon, we merge night with day.

Moonlit Reveries

Under a sky of silver hue,
Dreams awaken, soft and true.
Whispers float on gentle breeze,
Carried through the swaying trees.

Shadows dance on fields of night,
Guided by the pale moonlight.
Hearts entwined in quiet bliss,
In the dark, we find our kiss.

Memories wrapped in tender rays,
Floating thoughts of brighter days.
Stars above, like scattered dreams,
Illuminate our secret schemes.

In this reverie, time stands still,
Every moment, a precious thrill.
Together lost in whispers sweet,
Where night and day seamlessly meet.

The Hour of Forgotten Fantasies

In the stillness of the night,
Whispers beckon out of sight.
Chasing shadows, lost in thought,
Time slips by, a fleeting knot.

Hidden dreams from long ago,
Surface softly, like the snow.
Every sigh, a story told,
In the dark, secrets unfold.

Faded wishes, distant calls,
Echo softly through the halls.
As the hour grows ever late,
We discover what we create.

In the cradle of the night,
Resting dreams take gentle flight.
Binding dreams with threads of gold,
In this hour, brave and bold.

Starlit Pathways of Memory

Beneath a tapestry of stars,
We wander past both near and far.
Through the corridors of time,
Sweet reflections, soft as rhyme.

Footsteps whispered on the ground,
In each echo, love is found.
Every star, a tale awakes,
Guiding us through memories' lakes.

Moments sketched in silver light,
Painted dreams that feel so right.
As we stroll this winding way,
Past and present gently play.

With each breath, the night renews,
In the dark, we find our views.
Starlit pathways draw us near,
To the places we hold dear.

Beneath the Canopy of Slumber

Cradled softly in the night,
Dreams unfold like wings in flight.
Underneath the velvet dome,
Hearts discover a hidden home.

In this realm where silence sings,
The soul learns what dreaming brings.
With each sigh, the spirit soars,
Unlocking all the unseen doors.

Whispers of the night express,
Gentle hopes and pure caress.
Beneath the stars' watchful eyes,
Lies the truth where comfort lies.

Wrapped in warmth, we drift away,
Through the night until the day.
In slumber's grace, we find our rest,
In dreams, we are truly blessed.

Reflections in the Deep Blue Dark

Beneath the stars, the waters sigh,
Ripples dance where dreams float nigh.
Whispers weave through the silent night,
Echoes linger, soft and light.

Shadows swirl in a gentle maze,
Moonlight spills in silver rays.
Thoughts submerge in the tranquil tide,
Hidden feelings swell inside.

Quiet moments, secrets kept,
In the depths, emotions wept.
Time unraveled, softly spun,
Reflections fade, yet still they run.

Celestial Soliloquy

In the expanse where silence weaves,
Stars converse, their light deceives.
Galaxies twirl in cosmic grace,
Each heartbeat marks a sacred space.

Whispers drift on solar winds,
Echoing tales where time rescinds.
Constellations share their dreams,
Painting paths with vibrant gleams.

Planets hum in rhythmic tune,
Underneath the watchful moon.
Every twinkle tells a tale,
Of time and love that will not fail.

The Hidden Garden of Sleep

In the twilight where shadows bloom,
Petals whisper, dispelling gloom.
Dreams emerge from softly spun,
Mysteries rest till day is done.

Moonbeams grace the tranquil ground,
Among the blooms, peace is found.
Silken threads of night enfold,
Secrets blossom, dreams unfold.

Voices hush in gentle sighs,
As twilight paints the velvet skies.
A haven waits with open charms,
Embraced in night's soft, loving arms.

Whispers of the Darkened Hour

When the world slips into night,
Silent echoes claim their flight.
S shadows breathe a soft refrain,
Secrets held in softest pain.

Time stands still in muted grace,
As dreams unveil their hidden face.
Each heartbeat thuds, a gentle plea,
In the dark, we cease to flee.

Mysteries dance on velvet streams,
Carried softly, woven dreams.
A chorus hums, the shadows play,
In the night where spirits sway.

Reflections in the Dark

Shadows whisper tales untold,
In the quiet, secrets fold.
Echoes dance with silent grace,
Time reveals a hidden face.

Stars flicker in the night sky,
Silent witnesses, they lie.
Moments fade, yet linger near,
In the dark, we face our fear.

Heartbeats sync with twilight's breath,
Life's reflections dance with death.
Underneath the velvet hue,
Thoughts return to shades of blue.

In solitude, we find our way,
Guided by the light of day.
What is lost shall be restored,
In the calm, our spirits soared.

Enigmas of the Starry Veil

Beneath the sky of midnight's grace,
Secrets weave in endless space.
Galaxies in silent tune,
Whisper stories under the moon.

Constellations draw their lines,
In the dark, the mystery shines.
Celestial bodies blink and sway,
Holding dreams that drift away.

Through the veil of starlit dreams,
Questioning what silence means.
Every shimmer holds a spark,
Filling voids within the dark.

In the twilight's tender glow,
We seek answers, yet don't know.
Within the cosmic dance we stride,
Finding peace where wonders hide.

Fantasia in the Quiet Hours

When the world is hush and still,
Dreams awaken, soft and shrill.
Imagination takes its flight,
In the calm of fall's twilight.

Whispers echo on the breeze,
Carrying tales among the trees.
Colors blend in twilight's art,
Painting musings on the heart.

Memories drift like fragrant air,
In the night, we're free from care.
Fables spun in silver light,
Guiding hearts through endless night.

In these hours, we gently sway,
Caught in dreams that stretch and play.
Lost in worlds both bright and grand,
Finding magic in the sand.

Moonbeams and Midnight Musings

Moonbeams dance on silver streams,
Casting light on sleepy dreams.
Midnight whispers softly call,
In these moments, we stand tall.

Thoughts meander like a brook,
In the shadows, wisdom's took.
Every sigh a secret song,
In the night where souls belong.

Glistening stars like eyes appear,
Holding wishes close and dear.
Through the veil of night we roam,
In this darkness, we find home.

Gentle night, a compass bright,
Guiding hearts with sweet delight.
In the stillness, truth unfolds,
Wrapped in dreams and moonlit gold.

Echoes of a Hushed Heart

In shadows soft, where secrets dwell,
A timid heart begins to swell.
Whispers dance on the still night air,
Echoes of love, both sweet and rare.

Lonely stars gleam in silence deep,
Guarding dreams that softly creep.
Each beat within, a tale untold,
Of fragile hopes and hearts of gold.

Time drifts like clouds across the sky,
Casting light on nights gone by.
In every sigh, a promise made,
In every tear, a vow displayed.

Yet still we linger, lost in thought,
For every love, a lesson taught.
In echoes sweet, we find our way,
Through the hush of night, to break of day.

Beneath the Twilight Whisper

Beneath the glow where shadows play,
The twilight whispers come to stay.
Colors blend in a soft embrace,
Night unfolds with a tender grace.

Silhouettes dance on the fading light,
Stars awaken, banishing night.
Dreamers dream on a velvet sea,
Carried softly, where hearts are free.

In this realm where time stands still,
Hope intertwines with the night's chill.
Every murmur, a secret shared,
In the silence, souls are bared.

As night bequeaths its gentle kiss,
We weave a tapestry of bliss.
Beneath the twilight, shadows sway,
A magic world, where we can play.

Celestial Slumbers

Up in the sky where the stars gleam,
A cosmic dance, a fleeting dream.
Planets spin in their silent flight,
Guided gently by the moonlight.

Each twinkle tells a story old,
Of lovers lost and hearts of gold.
In this vastness, we close our eyes,
To hear the whispers of the skies.

Clouds drift softly, wrapped in night,
Embracing all in tender light.
Slumbers deep with wishes sown,
In cosmic fields, we are not alone.

Dreamers wander through endless space,
Finding solace in time and place.
In celestial arms, we drift away,
Forever held in the Milky Way.

Chasing the Moonlit Breeze

Underneath the nightly sheen,
We chase the whispers, soft and keen.
Moonlit paths are calling near,
With every heart, we'll persevere.

Branches sway with stories old,
In the night where dreams unfold.
Every breeze, a gentle song,
Carrying hopes, where we belong.

Footprints lead through silent glades,
Where light and shadow gently fades.
In the stillness, wild hearts race,
Chasing the moon's enchanting grace.

Together we roam, hand in hand,
Exploring the magic of this land.
For in the night, we are alive,
Chasing dreams that help us thrive.

Nocturnal Ballet of the Mind

In shadows deep, the thoughts take flight,
Whispers twirl in the cloak of night.
Dreams entwined, they gracefully sway,
A dance unfolds till break of day.

Stars above, a silent audience,
Each twinkle is a secret, dense.
Mind's theater, a curious show,
As night casts its enchanting glow.

Flickers spark in the brain's vast sea,
Chasing visions wild and free.
With every leap, they flirt and tease,
A ballet bound by night's warm breeze.

In the hush, ideas pirouette,
A nocturnal waltz, never to forget.
Till dawn arrives, they take their bow,
The mind's grand show concludes somehow.

The Mysterious Tides of Twilight

Beneath the dimming sky's embrace,
Waves of dusk in gentle grace.
Shadows dance on the ocean's edge,
Secrets whispered from the ledge.

Moonlight drapes like silver lace,
Casting spells in a tranquil space.
With each breath, the world does sigh,
As stars ignite in the velvet sky.

The horizon blurs, a dreamy blend,
Where day and night begin to mend.
The tides they ebb, the colors merge,
Crafting dreams as they emerge.

In twilight's hold, we drift away,
On waves of wonder, hearts at play.
A moment caught, forever stays,
In the tide's mysterious ways.

Sleep's Enchanted Canvas

An artist drapes the world in night,
With softest strokes, a pure delight.
Dreams are painted in shades of gray,
On sleep's canvas, they gently sway.

Stars become the spark and hue,
Brush of moonlight, silver dew.
In tranquil scenes, our hearts reside,
As slumber's magic does abide.

Imagined realms where fantasies grow,
Like rivers flowing, steady and slow.
Each vision blooms in vibrant tides,
As sleep takes us on endless rides.

With night's embrace, we find our peace,
In artful moments that never cease.
The canvas breathes the dreams we weave,
In slumber's realm, we learn to believe.

Veils of the Midnight Muse

In the stillness where echoes hum,
The muse arrives, a gentle drum.
Veiled in shadows, she softly gleams,
Igniting hearts with whispered dreams.

Midnight's chill, a sacred space,
Fingers dance in poetic grace.
Words like stars in the velvet night,
Illuminate thoughts, pure and bright.

In the quiet, inspiration flows,
With every breath, the soul bestows.
Veils of magic, they shimmer and sway,
Guiding the lost on their way.

With ink and heart, we craft and weave,
The midnight muse, we gladly receive.
In the depth of night, our spirits soar,
Unlocking worlds forevermore.

The Canvas of Midnight's Heart

Stars paint whispers on the dark,
Dreams emerge with a gentle spark.
Each shadow dances, a fleeting sigh,
As time drifts softly, the moments fly.

Colors fade like the evening light,
Secrets hidden in the heart's delight.
Midnight's brush strokes a tale so old,
Every heartbeat, a story told.

In the silence, echoes resound,
Fragments of love in stillness found.
With every breath, the canvas glows,
Painting life as the starlight flows.

Veils of night weave a mystic thread,
Lifting the soul where spirits tread.
In the depth of dark, we learn to be,
The canvas of our hearts set free.

Light and Shadow Intertwined

In the twilight where day meets night,
Shadows gather, soft and light.
A dance of hues in the fading sun,
Whispers of dreams where there's no run.

Brightened corners cradle the dark,
As hope ignites a gentle spark.
Each silhouette tells a tale of grace,
In the embrace of a transient space.

Fleeting glimmers break the gloom,
Where laughter lingers, flowers bloom.
Light and shadow in unity play,
Creating magic in the fray.

Hearts intertwined like the branches up high,
A tapestry woven with each gentle sigh.
In the play of contrast, we find our way,
The canvas of life in vibrant array.

Fantasies Adrift in the Moonlight

Beneath the silver glow we dream,
Soft whispers dance on a gentle stream.
Fantasies twirl on a midnight breeze,
Carried away with the rustling trees.

Stars like secrets dot the skies,
Reflecting hopes in our sleeping eyes.
With every breath, the night unfolds,
A tapestry of wonders, bright and bold.

Luminous paths lead us away,
To hidden worlds where shadows play.
In the embrace of the cool night air,
Stories awaken without a care.

Lost in the magic of the night's embrace,
Fantasies linger in a timeless space.
Adrift in dreams, our spirits soar,
As the moonlight calls us to explore.

Ocean of Night's Emotions

Waves crash softly on shores of time,
Whispers of feelings in rhythm and rhyme.
The ocean breathes, both wild and tame,
Carrying echoes of love's sweet name.

Tides pull gently at the heart's string,
Each ebb and flow, a sweet offering.
In the night's embrace, the waters sway,
Reflecting stars in an endless play.

Fading whispers of fading light,
In the depths of darkness, we find our sight.
The ocean stirs with tales untold,
Of memories treasured, and moments bold.

Upon the sands where dreams are born,
The ocean of night, a soft adorn.
In its embrace, emotions glide,
A journey taken, a world wide.

Nightfall's Enchantment

The sky draped in velvet deep,
Stars awaken from their sleep.
Whispers of the night begin,
Magic in the air we spin.

Moonlight dances on the ground,
Soft and gentle, all around.
Shadows play in corners bright,
As we bask in silvered light.

Dreams take flight on whispered winds,
Where the night and silence blend.
In this realm of mystic grace,
Time stands still, a warm embrace.

Hearts entwined beneath the sky,
In the dark, we learn to fly.
Nightfall weaves its wondrous thread,
With each star, a story spread.

Lullabies of the Dusk

As the sun begins to wane,
Softly hums the evening's strain.
Colors blend in sweet decline,
Nature sings her sweet design.

Crickets chirp in rhythmic songs,
Echoing where the night prolongs.
Gentle breezes through the trees,
Carry whispers on the breeze.

Dusk embraces all that's near,
Holding close what we hold dear.
In this hour, dreams take flight,
Lullabies of tender night.

Close your eyes and drift away,
Let the night lead you to play.
In the cradle of the dark,
Find the peace, let life embark.

Visions Beneath the Veil of Night

In the deep where shadows dwell,
Secrets woven, tales to tell.
Starlit skies, a canvas wide,
Whispered dreams we seek to hide.

Murmurs of the dark arise,
Glimmers dance in hidden skies.
Each flicker brings a thought anew,
Visions blur in shades of blue.

Beneath the veil, our hearts explore,
Finding paths we longed for more.
Mysteries in silence bloom,
In the night, we find our room.

With each breath, the world awakes,
In the dark, the magic breaks.
Let your spirit roam and glide,
In the night, let dreams provide.

Secrets Unraveled in the Gloom

Hushed and quiet, secrets keep,
In the twilight, shadows creep.
Beneath the stars, the truth unfolds,
In the dark, a tale retold.

Nighttime whispers, soft and low,
Where the gentle moonlight flows.
Each corner hides a mystery,
A world wrapped in history.

Lost in thought, we wander wide,
Through the hush, our dreams confide.
Glimpses of what lies ahead,
In the gloom, our fears are fed.

With each sigh, a truth revealed,
In the night, our hearts are healed.
Secrets woven, shadows loom,
In the dark, we find our room.

Visions Adrift in the Gloom

In the haze where shadows play,
Memories linger, soft and gray.
Echoes of dreams, fleeting and thin,
Whispers of where it might have been.

Silent footsteps on the ground,
Lost in thoughts that swirl around.
Images fade like morning mist,
Moments cherished, hard to resist.

Stars above in muted light,
Guide the weary through the night.
Nostalgia wraps like a gentle shawl,
Holding the heart, embracing all.

In the gloom, a vision gleams,
Carrying tales of silent dreams.
Hearts adrift, no safe harbor found,
Searching for solace in shadowed sound.

Night's Secret Symphony

In the dark where secrets brew,
Melodies whisper, pure and true.
A song of night begins to rise,
Cradling hearts beneath the skies.

Rustling leaves in gentle sway,
Nature's chorus, night's ballet.
Stars twinkle in harmonious tune,
While shadows dance beneath the moon.

Softly now, the world unfolds,
With stories waiting to be told.
Every heartbeat lends a rhyme,
Creating echoes lost in time.

Embrace the night, feel the flow,
Let the secret music grow.
In twilight's grasp, let spirits soar,
For in the dark, there's so much more.

Whispers of the Moonlit Hour

Beneath the glow, the night awakes,
As silver beams the silence breaks.
Whispers weave through tranquil skies,
Carrying secrets, ancient sighs.

In shadowed corners, dreams take flight,
As the world surrenders to night.
Each flicker of stars, a soft caress,
In the moon's embrace, we find our rest.

Night blooms with rhythm, soft and clear,
A tranquil heartbeat, drawing near.
Each moment lingers, a tender pause,
As time unwinds without a cause.

Underneath the moon's warm glow,
Whispers of love gently flow.
In this hour, a magic rare,
We lose ourselves in dreams to share.

Shadows Dance Beneath Starlit Skies

As night descends, the shadows play,
In a waltz with stars that sway.
Each movement speaks of tales untold,
Beneath the skies, both young and old.

Glimmers of light, so far away,
Guide the lost with gentle ray.
In the stillness, magic breathes,
Life reclaims its woven wreaths.

The calm of night heals aching hearts,
Removing broken, frayed parts.
A dance of hope against the gloom,
Where love and peace are bound to bloom.

In shadows deep, the spirits twine,
Crafting dreams in the moon's design.
Under starlit skies, we find our way,
Dancing forever, night and day.

Veil of Stardust Whispers

In the quiet of the night, soft dreams flow,
Veils of silver glimmer, where wishes grow.
Whispers of stardust dance in the air,
Carried by breezes, gentle and rare.

Beneath the vast canopy of the dark,
Echoes of secrets ignite a spark.
Flickering lights weave tales of the past,
In this cosmic embrace, moments last.

Floating amidst a sea of bright hues,
Each twinkle a promise, each glimmer, a muse.
Voices of galaxies call from afar,
Reminding us softly, we're never ajar.

So let us drift in this dreamy delight,
Grasping the whispers that shimmer at night.
In the cloak of the cosmos, hearts intertwine,
Wrapped in the magic where dreams brightly shine.

Shadows Paint the Sky

As daylight fades, shadows softly creep,
Painting the sky where silence will seep.
Colors of twilight blend and entwine,
Crafting a canvas that feels so divine.

Beneath the horizon, whispers take flight,
Echoes of dusk herald the coming night.
Stars awaken, their secrets unspool,
Illuminating the quiet, a mystical rule.

In the embrace of evening's final breath,
Shadows stretch long, hinting at death.
Yet life persists in the whispers of gold,
A promise that dusk is simply foretold.

So linger a while in this painted expanse,
Where shadows and light play a delicate dance.
Each moment a flicker of beauty to pass,
As night envelopes, like a velveted glass.

Lullabies of the Silver Moon

A silver moon glows in a tranquil sea,
Lullabies echo, sweet as can be.
Softly they drift on the cool, gentle breeze,
Hushing the world, bringing hearts to ease.

Crickets serenade in the hush of the night,
Chanting their melodies, pure and bright.
Stars twinkle softly, keeping time's beat,
As dreams intertwine in a dance discreet.

Whispers of night caress weary souls,
Filling the silence, making us whole.
The fabric of slumber, woven with care,
Wraps us in comfort, light as the air.

So close your eyes under the moon's silver glow,
Let the lullabies guide you, where peace flows.
In the heart of the dark, find solace and rest,
In the arms of the night, feel truly blessed.

Nocturnal Serenade

Under a blanket of darkness so deep,
Nature unfolds in a hush, whispers creep.
A nocturnal serenade begins to play,
Harmonies fill the night, guiding the stray.

The rustle of leaves and the croon of the night,
Echo tales of the woodland, pure and light.
Each swaying branch sings a song of the old,
In the embrace of night, mysteries unfold.

Owl's haunting call meets the softest breeze,
As shadows move gracefully, dancing through trees.
Crickets conduct an orchestra, sweet and low,
Their rhythm a heartbeat, a soft undertow.

In this symphony woven with silken threads,
The pulse of the evening where silence spreads.
So linger a moment and let your heart sway,
With the nocturnal serenade's gentle display.

Symphony of Softly Fallen Stars

In the night, stars softly fall,
Whispers of dreams that call and enthrall.
They dance on whispers, pure and bright,
Guiding the souls through the velvet night.

A melody hums on the gentle breeze,
Carrying secrets from ancient trees.
Each twinkle a note, each glow a refrain,
In the symphony felt, joy mingles with pain.

Time drifts like clouds in the twilight glow,
Painting the skies with promises aglow.
As shadows fade, hopes rise anew,
In this cosmic concert, our hearts find their hue.

So let us gather where starlight pours,
Chasing the echoes through celestial doors.
In the quiet embrace of night's soft art,
We find the rhythm that lives in our heart.

Dreams Woven in Starbursts

In a tapestry spun from glowing skies,
Dreams unfurl as the day softly dies.
Each star a thread, each pulse a story,
Whirling in cosmic dance, weaving glory.

Bright bursts of light, like hope in despair,
Carving the shadows, a puzzle laid bare.
Within their glow lies a truth so deep,
As they whisper to us while we peacefully sleep.

Threads of wishes, stitched with care,
Crafting a world where love can repair.
Every heartbeat, a spark in the dark,
Guided by starlight, igniting the spark.

In the realm where the celestial roams,
We find our way, feeling at home.
Dreams woven tight in a vibrant chart,
Connecting the heavens to each longing heart.

Ciphers of the Starry Night

In the ink of night, secrets unfold,
Ciphers of stars, stories untold.
Each shimmer a clue in the darkened sky,
Whispering truths as the galaxies sigh.

Galaxies spin in a dance, so divine,
Writing their tales in the cosmos' line.
Deciphering patterns, we gaze with wonder,
Revealing the mysteries hidden in thunder.

Constellations twinkle, painting the dark,
Drawing our eyes to their delicate spark.
Captured in twilight, hopes take flight,
In the puzzle of dreams that fill the night.

So take my hand as we venture between,
Past the known worlds where none have seen.
In the ciphers that guide us, let's find delight,
Together we roam through the starry night.

Traces of Celestial Whispers

Softly they linger, celestial sounds,
Whispers of stardust in twilight grounds.
Echoes of wishes, gentle and clear,
Carried by breezes, they cool every tear.

Each note a promise, swaying in time,
Celestial pages, a rhythm, a rhyme.
Fleeting yet endless, in moments they float,
On threads of the cosmos, our spirits emote.

In the silence of night, these whispers reside,
Wrapping the earth in a warm, glowing tide.
Traces of dreams shimmer, fading away,
Leaving their warmth as they gently sway.

So listen intently, for they hold the key,
To unlock the wonders of what's yet to be.
In the embrace of the night, let them unfurl,
Tracing the path in this cosmic swirl.

Heartbeats in the Midnight Hour

In the quiet of night, whispers flow,
Softly swaying like shadows below.
A rhythm so gentle, it sings in our soul,
Heartbeats in sync, making us whole.

Stars twinkle down with a knowing light,
Guiding our thoughts through the stillness of night.
Beyond all the worries, the world fades away,
In the heart of the moment, we choose to stay.

Breaths intertwine in a dance so sweet,
Lost in a dream where our spirits meet.
The clock strikes on, yet we linger still,
Wrapped in this magic, a timeless thrill.

As dawn starts to break, our shadows will part,
But the night's gentle song will stay in our heart.
Together we ventured through dark and through light,
In the echoes of love, we'll meet again bright.

Echoes of Silent Longings

Beneath the surface, the whispers reside,
In chambers of longing where secrets abide.
Each breath is a prayer, a hope in the air,
For voices unspoken still linger with care.

In the twilight hush, where shadows convene,
A symphony plays of what might have been.
The heart beats a melody, soft yet profound,
In echoes of silence, our truths can be found.

Every glance holds a weight too heavy to bear,
In delicate moments, we're stripped and laid bare.
With wishes like petals, we'll scatter and drift,
Carried by dreams, our hearts gently lift.

Yet still in the quiet, where wishes take flight,
We cherish the echoes that dance in the night.
For every unspoken, a feeling remains,
In the depth of our silence, true longing sustains.

The Magic of Shadowed Dreams

In the corners of night, where shadows extend,
A realm comes alive where dreams can transcend.
We wander through vistas of shimmering light,
In the magic of dreams that unfold out of sight.

Each whispering breeze carries tales of the heart,
As flickers of stardust weave worlds set apart.
Through portals of slumber, we chase the divine,
On the canvas of night, where all paths align.

With every soft sigh, a new journey starts,
In the lull of the night, we awaken our hearts.
With eyes gently closed, we embrace the unknown,
In the magic of dreams, we are never alone.

As dawn softly steals, and shadows recede,
The threads of our dreams become visions we need.
Though fleeting they seem, they echo and glow,
In the depths of our souls, their magic will flow.

Serene Reflections Under Stardust

In the stillness of night, beneath starlit skies,
We gather our thoughts, as the world gently sighs.
Reflecting on moments that shaped who we are,
With love as our compass, we gaze at each star.

Waves of tranquility wash over our minds,
In this sacred space, where silence unwinds.
The beauty of life rests in innocent grace,
As we find our place in the cosmos' embrace.

With every twinkling, a story unfolds,
The whispers of stardust, a treasure to hold.
In the quiet of night, dreams softly align,
In the serenity found, our hearts intertwine.

As we drift through the hours, in peace we remain,
Under velvet skies, where love knows no pain.
Together we'll wander, forever we've known,
In the starlit reflections, we're never alone.

Echoes of Midnight Reveries

In shadows deep, the whispers sigh,
Dreams take flight, beneath the sky.
Silken threads of starlit grace,
Float like ghosts in a secret place.

Time stands still, as moments blend,
Memories dance, and hearts transcend.
The night unfolds, a canvas wide,
Where secrets of the soul abide.

Moonlight spills on quiet streams,
Cradling softly our midnight dreams.
In the hush of the darkened air,
Magic lingers, everywhere.

Awake we wander, lost yet found,
In the echoes, a haunting sound.
With every breath, the night inspires,
A symphony of heart's desires.

The Secrets that Twilight Keeps

As daylight fades, the shadows creep,
Twilight dances, secrets deep.
In the glow of the setting sun,
Whispers stir, the stories run.

Colors blend in a painter's hand,
Shifting dreams across the land.
Velvet skies hold tales untold,
Of hidden paths and hearts of gold.

The horizon breathes a sigh of peace,
In this moment, worries cease.
Stars awaken with gentle light,
Guardians of the coming night.

With every spark, a wish ignites,
In twilight's grasp, the soul delights.
Secrets linger in the air,
For those who seek, and those who dare.

Murmurs of the Nocturnal Heart

Beneath the cloak of starlit skies,
The nocturnal heart softly lies.
With every beat, a whisper flows,
In moonlit dreams, where time bestows.

The nightingale sings a lover's tune,
In serenades to the silver moon.
Echoing through the slumbering trees,
The gentle sigh of a midnight breeze.

Secrets shared in tender space,
Intimate shadows, a soft embrace.
In quiet corners, our hopes align,
Murmurs of hearts, a sweet design.

Awakening sights in the dark's domain,
Where love is whispered, free from pain.
In silence rich, emotions spark,
Murmurs linger, igniting the dark.

Fantasies in Darkness

In the depth of night's embrace,
Fantasies find their sacred place.
Dreams unravel, like threads of light,
In the heart of endless night.

Shadows waltz beneath the stars,
Whispers linger from afar.
In the canvas of the unseen,
Worlds are born, a vibrant sheen.

Glimmers of hope in the midnight air,
Carried on winds of a silent prayer.
Eyes closed tight, the soul will roam,
Finding solace, far from home.

In darkness deep, we lose control,
Fantasies weave into the soul.
Embrace the night, let the spirit soar,
In the world of dreams, forever explore.

Fragments of Dusk's Lullaby

As twilight descends, dreams start to sway,
Silent whispers echo, fading away.
Shadows stretch long, embracing the light,
Dusk cradles the world, gently tucking tight.

Stars pierce the veil, like secrets untold,
In the heart of the night, the universe unfolds.
Each breath of the breeze brings soft, tender sighs,
Dusk sings a lullaby, where silence flies.

Night's canvas is painted with strokes of deep blue,
Each fragment a memory, each shimmer a cue.
As night creatures stir, in harmony, they play,
Together they weave the end of the day.

Bathed in the glow of a soft, silver hue,
Fragments of dusk remind me of you.
In the quiet embrace, where wishes are spun,
The lullaby beckons, as day is undone.

The Heartbeat of the Night

In the velvet dark, a rhythm untamed,
The pulse of the night, quietly named.
Each tick of the clock, a whisper below,
Echoes of secrets the shadows bestow.

Moonlight filters softly, a tender caress,
Nurturing dreams in a gentle finesse.
Stars flicker in time, like distant heartbeats,
A song of the cosmos, where silence repeats.

The air thick with magic, electric and bright,
Alluring enchantments dance in the night.
Every creature awake, caught in the flow,
The heartbeat of night has much to bestow.

Fleeting moments flare, then fade like the mist,
Yet they're stitched in the fabric of things we can't resist.
The symphony plays as we drift and we sway,
In the arms of the night, we long to stay.

Whispered Hopes Under the Dark Sky

Beneath a vast dome of glittering dreams,
Whispers of hopes rise like soft, silver beams.
Each star a promise, a wish in the night,
Guiding lost souls toward paths filled with light.

The cool breeze carries tales of the past,
Fragments of laughter, shadows that last.
Gentle reminders of moments held dear,
As whispers of hopes float, crystal clear.

Cloaked in the darkness, we gather our fears,
Transforming them slowly to rivers of tears.
Yet through the stillness, a flicker ignites,
Whispered hopes bloom in the heart of the night.

As constellations align in the void,
Dreams once elusive, no longer destroyed.
Together we stand, beneath this vast sky,
Whispered hopes echo, never asking why.

Stars Weaving Through the Silence

In the tapestry of night, stars gently weave,
Threads of starlight in silence, we believe.
Each glimmering point tells tales of afar,
Guiding our hearts like a cosmic memoir.

The heavens conspire in the hush of the hour,
A dance of the old, a bloom of new power.
As darkness embraces, stories unfold,
Stars whisper secrets of ages untold.

Wrapped in the silence, dreams intertwine,
Woven together, like patterns divine.
Each heartbeat finds rhythm, a silvery thread,
Stars weaving our souls, in the whispers of bread.

The night sky invites us to ponder and gaze,
Amidst the quiet, lost in a daze.
As we chase the shadows, forever we yearn,
Stars' soft illumination, a beacon to turn.

The Storyteller of the Dark

In shadows deep, a tale unfolds,
Whispers of secrets, ancient and bold.
The fire crackles, casting light,
As dreams take flight on this velvet night.

With every word, the night draws near,
A haunted echo, laced with fear.
From dusty tomes, the stories spring,
Of lost horizons and forgotten kings.

A flicker of hope in the stories told,
Of brave hearts wrought from threads of gold.
Yet in the silence where darkness swells,
The storyteller weaves his spells.

So gather close, let the tale ignite,
For in the dark, the magic's bright.
With each chapter, a world reborn,
The storyteller whispers until the dawn.

Refrains of Night's Poetry

In the stillness, the night does sing,
Gentle verses, soft winds bring.
Moonlight dances on dewy grass,
Through whispers of time, the moments pass.

Stars are the notes, scattered and bright,
Together they form the refrains of night.
In shadows, where silence weaves,
The heart finds peace, the spirit grieves.

Each breath a line, a melody sweet,
Where echoes of dreams and memories meet.
In twilight's arms, we find our place,
Lost in the rhythm, the night's embrace.

So listen close, and let it flow,
The poetry of night, as soft as snow.
In the quiet, let your soul take flight,
In the sweet refrains of the velvet night.

Sailing Through Oblivion

On waves of silence, we drift afar,
Bound to the whim of a distant star.
In the ether, a longing stirs,
With currents unseen, our fate occurs.

Time unravels in the twilight haze,
A journey lost in a nebulous maze.
With sails of thought, we brave the unknown,
In the depths, seeds of dreams are sown.

The horizon blurs, a canvas of night,
Where shadows dance in the fading light.
In whispers of wind, the ancients call,
Guiding our path through the darkness' thrall.

So sail we shall, through oblivion's sea,
With hearts as compass, wild and free.
For in the vast void, our spirits soar,
To find the shores we've yearned for more.

Midnight's Crimson Breath

In the hush of night, a moment gleams,
Crimson whispers weave through dreams.
The moon, a watchful guardian bright,
Holds secrets tight in the fabric of night.

With each breath drawn, a story swells,
Of fleeting hopes and magic spells.
In shadowed corners, the echoes play,
Where hearts beat softly, chasing the gray.

Through mist we wander, souls intertwined,
Seeking the light that destiny binds.
In midnight's arms, we find our grace,
As time dissolves in this sacred space.

So linger close, beneath the star's thread,
In crimson dreams where all is said.
For in that breath, the world transforms,
An endless dance in a heart that warms.

Starlit Fantasia

Beneath the sky of shimmering lights,
Dreams dance on the breeze of nights.
Whispers of stories long untold,
In the starlit arms, our hearts unfold.

A gentle glow on the horizon glows,
Magic flows where the cosmos knows.
Galaxies spin in a velvet sea,
Each twinkle a wish, wild and free.

Lost in the dreams that the night imparts,
Filling our souls and binding our hearts.
We wander the paths of the celestial stream,
In this starlit fantasia, all is but a dream.

So take my hand, let's drift away,
To where the night and magic play.
Under the watchful eye of the moon,
In starlit fantasia, morning comes too soon.

Murmurs from Beyond the Veil

In the hush of the night, soft echoes sigh,
Murmurs whisper secrets as shadows fly.
Between the realms where spirits tread,
Ancient tales of the long since dead.

Glimmers of light play in the dark,
Inviting the dreams that spark and hark.
Voices from places we've yet to find,
A tapestry woven through space and time.

They call to us in fragmented tones,
From the echoes of life with their distant moans.
In the folds of the veil, the mystery deep,
A cosmic dance that lulls us to sleep.

Should you listen closely, you might just hear,
The love and the loss, the joy and the fear.
Murmurs that rise like the morning dew,
From beyond the veil, they beckon to you.

The Twilight Canvas

Brushstrokes of purple kiss the day,
As twilight whispers the sun away.
Colors blend in a lover's embrace,
A canvas evolving, an artist's grace.

Silhouettes dance as shadows expand,
With secret stories at our command.
The horizon ignites, a fiery glow,
In this twilight realm, time begins to slow.

Stars peep out, a sparkling review,
Painting the world in shades of blue.
Each moment hangs in the evening air,
A masterpiece crafted, beyond compare.

The twilight canvas, rich and bold,
Holds the mysteries that nature unfolds.
As night drapes its veil and dreams take flight,
In the quietude, we find our light.

Threads of a Midnight Tale

In the heart of night, where shadows dwell,
We weave our dreams with a silken spell.
Threads of history, stories entwined,
In the fabric of twilight, realities bind.

With every stitch, a memory flows,
A midnight tale that forever grows.
Fables and whispers in the moon's soft light,
Inviting our souls to take flight.

Each thread a journey, a path unknown,
In the realm of dreams, seeds are sown.
Whispers of love that echo and swell,
In the depths of night, weave your own spell.

So gather the threads, let your heart prevail,
Crafting a story, your midnight tale.
With each weaving, let your spirit soar,
In the magical twilight, forever explore.

Echoes Beneath a Blanket of Dark

Whispers glide through the night air,
Faint shadows pause in their roam.
Stars flicker with a distant glow,
While dreams weave a tapestry at home.

Silence holds a delicate sway,
Crickets sing a lullaby soft.
Moonlight dances on the ground,
In darkness, fears begin to lift.

Footsteps echo on the grass,
Paths untold in the whispering trees.
Above, the cosmos holds its breath,
As time flows gently like a breeze.

In this night where secrets blend,
I'll find solace in the calm.
Each heartbeat a soft reminder,
That stillness sings a knowing psalm.

Twilight's Gentle Embrace

The sun dips low in a purple sky,
Casting hues of gold and sighs.
Shadows stretch across the land,
Twilight whispers, time flies by.

A breeze carries the scent of pine,
Each leaf dancing in tranquil grace.
The world softens as light wanes,
Embracing night's warm, tender face.

Stars awaken, the night unfolds,
Moonbeams brush the sleepy earth.
In this hour where dreams abound,
Twilight cradles all with mirth.

Hold tight to moments that fade fast,
Each breath a memory to keep.
In twilight's gentle embrace,
Our souls find peace and softly sleep.

Secrets of the Midnight Realm

In shadows deep where silence dwells,
Whispered secrets softly call.
The moonlight unveils hidden tales,
Of dreams and memories, big and small.

Each star a keeper of long-lost lore,
Glimmers of hope in the vast unknown.
Midnight holds a mirror wide,
Reflecting paths we've never shown.

Winds carry stories on their breath,
As night unveils its mystic art.
In this realm where time stands still,
We find the echoes of the heart.

Step lightly through each secret door,
Embrace the shadows, let them guide.
In this midnight realm we wander,
Where dreams and reality collide.

A Dance with the Celestial Shadows

Underneath a starlit dome,
Shadows weave their ancient dance.
With each twirl, a story told,
In cosmic rhythm, souls romance.

The night sky calls and we respond,
Boundless realms within our reach.
Each twinkle a beacon of hope,
Lessons from the stars they teach.

Galaxies swirl in a silent song,
Brushing dreams with a gentle hand.
In this waltz with shadowed light,
We find our place in the grand.

So dance with me, dear friend of night,
Let the universe embrace our fate.
For in the shadows, we belong,
In this dance, we celebrate.

Cradle of Moonshine Dreams

In the cradle where soft moonlight glows,
Dreams untangle like wind-kissed bows.
Whispers linger in the silky air,
As shadows dance without a care.

Night wraps the world in a gentle sigh,
While silver beams in silence lie.
A tapestry of wishes spun,
Under the gaze of the sleeping sun.

Crickets hum a lullaby sweet,
Guided by rhythms of heartbeats.
Stars twinkle like secrets shared,
With the night embracing those who dared.

In dreams we sail where the wild hearts roam,
Each moment a story, each breath a home.
In the cradle of night, our spirits soar,
As moonshine whispers forevermore.

The Silent Orchestra of Night

Under a cloak of midnight's grace,
The silent stars begin to trace.
A symphony in the dark unfolds,
With echoes of secrets, yet untold.

Winds play soft on the rustling leaves,
As nature weaves what the heart believes.
In the stillness, a rhythm flows,
Time stands still, as silence grows.

Moonlight stretches across the ground,
A conductor to dreams profound.
Each heartbeat a note, soft and clear,
In the orchestra that we all hear.

Whispers of shadows curl and sway,
In the music of night, we drift away.
With every breath, we share a part,
In the silent choir, we find our heart.

Dances of Stars and Shadows

In the twilight where echoes blend,
Stars and shadows begin to bend.
Whirling softly like leaves in flight,
A dance ignites the velvet night.

Golden glimmers kiss the floor,
As whispers twine, inviting more.
Footsteps trace a celestial map,
In this cosmic, gentle lap.

Every flicker, a story weaves,
In the embrace of hopes and dreams.
Shadows twirl, the moonlight beams,
In the climax of starlit schemes.

This ballet of light, a waltz so true,
Every moment crafted anew.
In the dance of the night, souls convene,
Where stars breathe life, and all is serene.

Whispers from the Abyss

From the depths where silence reigns,
Whispers float like soft, wild rains.
Secrets murmur in the dark deep,
Where shadows gather as spirits weep.

Echoes of time in the pitch-black sea,
Carried by winds that yearn to be free.
The abyss sings a haunting song,
Of lost dreams and where they belong.

In the twilight, reflections gleam,
Eldritch voices conjure a dream.
Each rippling wave, a tale retold,
Of love and loss, of brave and bold.

In the quiet, the heartbeats align,
Whispers from the abyss intertwine.
A lullaby sung by the dark below,
In the embrace of the night's soft glow.

Milton Keynes UK
Ingram Content Group UK Ltd.
UKHW021033021124
450589UK00013B/894

9 789916 905517